Living and Dying with Grace

Living & Dying with Grace

Counsels of ḤAḌRAT ʻALĪ

Translated from the Arabic

by THOMAS CLEARY

SHAMBHALA
Boston & London
1996

Shambhala Publications, Inc.
Horticultural Hall
300 Massachusetts Avenue
Boston, Massachusetts 02115
www.shambhala.com

Printed in the United States of America

Distributed in the United States by Random House, Inc.,
and in Canada by Random House of Canada Ltd

The Library of Congress catalogues the hardcover edition of this book as follows:

Sharīf al-Raḍī, Muḥammad ibn al-Ḥusayn, 969 or 70-1016.
[Nahj al-balāghah. English. Selections]
Living and dying with grace: counsels of Hadrat ʻAlī/translated from the Arabic by Thomas Cleary.—1st ed.
p. cm.
ISBN 1-57062-065-2
ISBN 1-57062-211-6 (paperback)
1. ʻAlī ibn Abī Ṭālib, Caliph, 600 (ca.)—661—Hadith. 2. Hadith (Shiites). I. Cleary, Thomas F., 1949– . II. Title.
BP193.1.A2S513 1995 94-43470
297′.1248—dc20 CIP
BVG 01

Translator's Introduction

Ḥaḍrat ("The Presence") 'Alī, who lived from 598 to 661 of the common era, was one of the greatest savants and leaders of early modern history. Artist and scholar, warrior and statesman, husband and father, Ḥaḍrat 'Alī is a traditional model for chivalry, learning, and devotion.

The father of 'Alī, Abū Ṭālib, was head of the House of Hāshim, a branch of the noble Arabian clan Quraish, custodians and priests of the august shrine of Mecca, believed to have been built by Abraham in antiquity. Abū Ṭālib was also the guardian of his ophaned nephew Muḥammad, who was to be instrumental in restoring the original religion of Abraham.

When Muḥammad began his prophetic mission, his young cousin 'Alī was one of the first to join him, and 'Alī's father, Abū Ṭālib, was one of those who protected and supported him against the fierce opposition of antagonistic members of the Quraish clan. 'Alī married the daughter of the Prophet Muḥammad and distinguished himself as a warrior in defense of the nascent religious community.

After the passing of Muḥammad the Prophet in 632,

'Alī did not seek leadership for himself but did assist and advise the Caliphs, or Successors, who followed the Prophet. 'Alī was offered the Caliphate in the third generation of succession, but did not take it. Only after the assassination of the third Caliph, in a time of division and confusion, did the great-hearted 'Alī accept the role of Commander of the Faithful. He thus became the fourth and last of the early Muslim leaders known as the Righteous Caliphs.

Through his spiritual companionship with the Prophet, 'Alī also inherited the transmission of deep knowledge associated with Islamic sainthood. Sufi masters consider 'Alī to be one of the Seven Great Ones in the first generation of classical teachers, and many of the Dervish orders trace their esoteric spiritual ancestry to 'Alī. Among the Shi'ah Muslims, 'Alī is revered as the first Imam, which means "leader" or "guide" and also "plumb line," that which shows the Straight Way.

The circumstances of his life exposed 'Alī to a vast range of experiences, which he absorbed and synthesized with the spirit and practice of faith, art, and science to produce a profound yet accessible understanding of life and death. This volume contains four hundred of Ḥaḍrat 'Alī's sayings translated from his famed *Nahj al-Balāgha,* "The Peak of Eloquence," a traditional model for classical Arabic diction and a luminous treasury of wisdom for living and dying with conscious grace.

Living and Dying with Grace

In times of unrest, be like a suckling calf,
which has no back to be ridden
and no udder to be milked.

Whoever is full of greed debases himself,
whoever reveals his distress accepts ignominy,
and whoever lets his tongue rule him
becomes despicable in his own eyes.

Avarice is destitution,
and cowardice is inadequacy.
Poverty gags the intelligent man,
preventing him from making his case,
while the pauper is a stranger in his own town.
Weakness is ruin,
while patience is valor.
Abstinence is wealth,
and caution is a shield.

The best of companions is contentment,
and knowledge is a noble, generous bequest.
Social graces are fresh clothing,
and meditation is a clear mirror.

The heart of an intelligent man is the vault of his secret.
Cheerfulness is the net of friendship.
Toleration is the tomb of imperfections,
and conciliation is the extinction of flaws.
And whoever is pleased with himself
increases resentment against him.

Charity is an effective medicine,
and the deeds of mortals in the temporal world
appear before their eyes
at the moment of their death.

When the world turns toward someone,
it lends him another's good,
and when it turns away from him,
it takes away his own good.

Associate with people in such a manner
that they weep for you when you die
and long for you if you are alive.

When you have overpowered an enemy,
show him forgiveness
out of gratitude for the ability to overpower him.

The biggest failures are those
who have failed to win friends,
but even bigger failures are those
who lose what friends they have made.

When little kindnesses come your way,
do not repel them by ingratitude.

To one whom the nearest deprive,
the most distant give.

No one who is obsessed is open to reproof.

All matters are subject to specific measures,
to the point where contrivance is fatal.

Whoever hurries with the reins of his expectation
stumbles because of it.

Fear is linked to failure
and timidity to deprivation,
and opportunity passes by like a cloud,
so take a good opportunity.

We have a right.
If it is given to us, fine;
but if not, we will take a backseat,
even if the night journey is long.

He whose action holds him back
is not to be promoted on account of his social status.

Whenever someone conceals anything,
it shows in slips of the tongue
and facial expressions.

Keep moving along when you are ailing,
to the extent you have any activity in you.

The most blessed abstinence
is concealment of abstinence.

When you are on the decline
and death is advancing,
what then?
The inevitable meeting
has accelerated its approach.

The doer of good is better than it is,
and the doer of evil is worse than it is.

Be generous without squandering,
appreciate value without being stingy.

The most noble wealth
is the relinquishment of objects of desire.

Whoever rushes to people
with what they do not like
is spoken of by them
in terms of what they do not know.

Whoever extends wishful thinking spoils action.

Ḥaḍrat 'Alī said to his son Ḥasan,
"My son, remember four things from me,
and four more;
you will come to no harm
as long as you act in accord with them.
The richest of riches is intelligence,
and the greatest poverty is stupidity.
The loneliest isolation is conceit,
and the most noble value is goodness of character.
My son, do not befriend a fool,
for he hurts you when he wants to help you.
And do not befriend a stingy man,
for he will distance himself from you
when he is most needed.
And do not befriend a profligate,
as he will sell you for a trifle.
And do not befriend a liar,
for he is like a mirage,
making the distant seem near to you
and the near seem distant."

The tongue of the intelligent man is behind his heart, whereas the heart of the fool is behind his intelligence.

The heart of the fool is in his mouth,
while the tongue of the intelligent man is in his heart.

The measure of a man depends
on the scope of his resolution,
and his sincerity depends
on the degree of his chivalric virtues.
His courage depends
on the degree of honor he has,
and his integrity is based
on the degree of his sense of shame.

Triumph comes about through resoluteness,
resoluteness comes through thinking ideas through,
and ideas come from keeping inmost thoughts
    inaccessible.

Beware of the tyranny
of the aristocrat
when he is hungry
and of the lowly one
when he is satiated.

Human hearts are brutish;
they take to whoever tames them.

Your shortcoming is concealed
as long as your luck helps you.

The foremost of people in forgiveness
is the most powerful of them in punishment.

Generosity is that which comes from one's own
initiative;
as for what is given in response to a request,
that is either shame or rebuke.

There is no wealth like intelligence
and no poverty like ignorance.
There is no heritage like culture
and no backup like consultation.

Patience is twofold:
patience in the face of what you dislike,
and patience in the absence of what you like.

The rich man is at home even when abroad;
the pauper is a stranger in his hometown.

Satisfaction is wealth that never runs out.

Wealth is the material constituent of yearnings.

One who cautions you
is as one who brings you good news.

The tongue is a wild beast;
when it is let loose, it wounds.

When you are greeted,
return an even nicer greeting,
and when you are done a service,
repay it with something even more,
though the blessing is with
the one who acted first.

The mediator is the wing of the seeker.

Adherents of the world are like a caravan
that leads them away even as they sleep.

Loss of a beloved is exile.

Neglect of needs is easier
than seeking them from strangers.

Do not be embarrassed
to give but a little,
for it is even less generous
to withhold altogether.

Purity is the ornament of the poor,
gratitude the ornament of the rich.

When what you seek
has not come about,
do not be concerned
about what you used to be.

You will find the ignorant
either remiss or excessive.

The more intelligence, the less talk.

Time wears out bodies
even as it renews hopes;
it brings death nearer
and removes aspiration.
Whoever takes advantage of it
becomes exhausted;
whoever lets it slip by toils.

Whoever sets himself up
as a leader of other people
should start educating himself
before educating others,
and let him teach by his conduct
before teaching by his tongue.
And the education and refinement
of one's self
is more worthy of respect
than the education and culture of other people.

Each breath one takes
is a step toward one's destiny.

Everything quantifiable
runs out,
and everything anticipated
is yet to come.

When things are unclear,
the later are seen in light of the earlier.

Lay hold of wisdom, wherever it is,
for wisdom stammers in the heart of a hypocrite
until it leaves and comes to rest by its like
in the heart of a believer.

A word of wisdom is the stray
of one who believes,
so lay hold of words of wisdom,
even if they come from hypocrites.

The worth of an individual
is what one does well.

When asked about what you do not know,
do not be ashamed to say you do not know;

and when you do not know something,
do not be embarrassed to learn it.
And may you have patience,
for patience is to faith
as the head is to the body;
there is no good in a body without its head,
and none in faith without patience.

Whoever gives up saying "I don't know"
has been mortally stricken.

The vision of an elder is dearer to me
than the endurance of a youth.

I marvel at one who despairs
while still able to seek forgiveness.

These hearts weary as the bodies weary,
so seek bits of wisdom for them.

Lower knowledge
is what stops at the tongue;

more elevated knowledge
is what is evident in the limbs and organs.

A conscientious act is not insignificant,
for how can what has been accepted be insignificant?

Understand information you hear
with the reasoning of responsibility
not the reasoning of the reporter,
for there are many reports of knowledge,
but few are responsible.

To fulfill needs is not sound
except under three conditions:
by considering it small,
that it may become great;
by concealing it,
that it may become apparent;
and by expediting it,
that it may be beneficial.

A time is coming to humankind
when none will be advanced
but the schemer,

and none will be adorned
but the profligate,
and none will be debased
but the just.
They will consider charity to be a loss,
loving-kindness in relationships to be a favor,
and worship to be arrogance before others.
In that time,
rulership will be through the counsel of women,
the authority of youths,
and the devices of eunuchs.

Many an intellectual
has been killed by his ignorance,
the knowledge he had with him
failing to profit him.

There is a part of a human being,
suspended by the aorta,
that is the strangest thing in there;
and that is the heart.
It has the friendship of wisdom
and opposition from what diverges therefrom:
when hope presents itself to it,
covetousness debases it;
when covetousness is stirred up by it,

that ruins endeavor.
When desperation ravages it,
regret kills it.
When anger appears in it,
irritation intensifies thereby.
When pleasure makes it happy,
it forgets reserve.
When fear comes upon it,
wariness keeps it preoccupied.
If security stretches all around,
heedlessness dispossesses it.
If it gets advantage from wealth,
affluence makes it overstep bounds.
If misfortune comes upon it,
anxiety violates it.
If neediness clings to it,
distress preoccupies it.
If hunger strains it,
that paralyzes it in feebleness.
If it goes too far in eating to satiety,
the gut is burdened.
So every deficiency is harmful to it,
and every excess is ruinous to it.

No wealth brings greater return than intelligence,
and no aloneness is more desolate than vanity.
There is no intelligence like good planning,

and no high-mindedness like conscience in awe of
Truth.
There is no companion like good-naturedness,
and no legacy like culture.
There is no leader like peacemaking,
and no business like good works.
There is no profit like recompense,
and no piety like stopping specious argument.
There is no abstinence like abstinence from the
forbidden,
and there is no knowledge like reflection.
There is no worship like discharge of obligations,
and no faith like modesty and patience.
There is no prestige like humility,
and no nobility like knowledge.
There is no power like clemency,
and no support surer than consultation.

When goodness has taken possession
of a time and its people,
if one entertains an evil supposition
about somebody who has evidenced nothing vile,
that is oppression.
And when perversity has taken possession
of a time and its people,
if one entertains a good opinion of somebody,
one is imperiled.

When asked how he was, Ḥaḍrat ʿAlī replied,
"How is one who consumes his existence,
falls sick when in health,
and is taken away from his place of safety?"

Two people are ruined on my account:
one who loves excessively,
and one who hates intensely.

Waste of an opportunity is torment.

The world is like a serpent,
soft to the touch but with poison inside.
The ignorant heedless one reaches for it,
while the intelligent one is wary of it.

What a difference there is between two actions:
an act whose pleasure departs
but whose consequence remains,
and an act whose difficulty departs
but whose reward remains.

Once Ḥaḍrat ʻAlī was following a funeral procession
when he heard someone laugh.
Ḥaḍrat ʻAlī said:
"As if death in this world were ordained only for others!
As if justice in this world were obligatory only on others!
As if those we see dying will return to us before long!
We put them in their graves
and enjoy what they have left behind,
as if we were going to be given immortality after them.
And we have forgotten every counselor, male and female,
and exposed ourselves to everything ruinous!"

Blessed is one
who is humble regarding himself,
whose livelihood is good,
whose inner thoughts are virtuous,
whose character is good,
who spends the surplus from his wealth
and removes superfluity from his speech,
who keeps his evil away from people,
who is sufficed by normalcy
and not involved in arbitrary invention.

Whoever falls short in action
is afflicted by uneasiness.

Protect yourself against cold when it begins
and welcome it at its end,
for it acts on bodies as it acts on trees:
at first it scorches and parches;
at the end it causes leaves to sprout.

Viewing graves outside of Kufa
on returning from the battle of Ṣiffīn,*
Ḥaḍrat ʻAlī said:
"O people of desolate abodes,
of empty shops,
of dark tombs!
O people of the dust,
O people of exile,
O people of isolation,
O people of gloom!
You went before us,
and we will follow after you.
As for your houses,
they have been occupied;
as for your spouses,
they have been remarried;

*The battle of Ṣiffīn was a prolonged conflict in an insurrection against ʻAlī's Caliphate by a would-be usurper. When ʻAlī eventually agreed on arbitration to prevent more bloodshed, a large group of old-time traditionalists abandoned him; these are called the Seceders.

and as for your wealth,
it has been distributed.
This is the news from where we are;
and what is the news where you are?"
Then Ḥaḍrat 'Alī turned to his companions and said:
"If they were allowed to talk,
they would tell you
the best provision
is conscience in awe of Truth."

Once when he heard someone
finding fault with the world, Ḥaḍrat 'Alī said:
"O you who revile the world,
blinded by its deceit,
duped by its falsehood!
Do you rebuke the world
after having been deluded by it?
Are you accusing it,
or is it accusing you?
When did it seduce you,
when did it beguile you?
Was it by the battlegrounds
where your fathers rot,
or the couches of your mothers
under the ground?
How much have you kept busy
seeing to their needs,

and how much have you personally
nursed them in illness?
You seek a remedy for them
and consult doctors for them.
On the morrow your treatment
will fail to benefit them,
your lament of no use to them,
your solicitude of no avail to any of them.
Your wish has not been granted,
and your power cannot defend them.
The world has given you thereby
an example of what will happen to you,
showing you your death
by means of the death of another.
In fact, the world is an abode of truth
for one who is truthful with it
and an abode of well-being
for one who understands it.
It is an abode of riches
for one who learns from it
and an abode of counsel
for one who takes a warning from it.
It is the house of worship
for those who love God,
the place of prayer of God's angels,
the place of descent of God's inspiration,
and the place of business of God's saints.
Therein is Mercy earned,

and therein is Paradise gained.
So who reviles it
when it has already announced its departure
and declared it would leave?
It has announced its own death
and that of its people;
by its trials
it has given them an example of tribulation,
and by its pleasures
filled them with longing for pleasure.
It started out with well-being
and created misfortune,
awakening desires and fears,
causing alarm and alert.
So some people revile it
on a morning of remorse,
while others will praise it
on the day of resurrection,
for the world reminded them
and they bore it in mind,
and it spoke to them
and they verified what it said,
and it cautioned them
and they took the warning."

The world is a transitory abode,
not a permanent abode.

And the people in it
are of two sorts:
one who sells his soul
and ruins it,
and one who ransoms his soul
and frees it.

A friend is not a true friend
unless he protects his brother
in three situations:
in his misfortune,
in his absence,
and at his death.

Beckon fortune by means of charity.

Whoever is sure of the outcome
is generous in giving.

One who is moderate
does not go wrong.

Having a small family
is one of two kinds of ease.

Friendliness is half of intelligence.

Sorrow is half of old age.

Patience comes down
according to misfortune,
so if anyone strikes his hand on his thigh
in his misfortune,
his work comes to naught.

A man is concealed under his tongue.

A man who does not know his measure is ruined.

To someone who asked for counsel,
Ḥaḍrat 'Alī said:
"Do not be one of those
who hope for the Hereafter without work,
and postpone repentance
by exaggeration of hope;
who speak in this world

the speech of the abstemious,
but work therein the work of the covetous;
who when given anything from it
are not satisfied,
and when forbidden anything from it
are discontent;
who are incapable of gratitude
for what they have been given,
and perpetually seek more and more;
who restrain others
but do not themselves abstain,
and command others to do
what they themselves do not;
who love the good
but not their works,
and despise sinners
while being sinners themselves;
who abhor death
because they have sinned too much,
yet persist in that for which they abhor death;
who become ruefully repentant when sick
and heedlessly confident when well;
who are proud when carefree
and despondent in times of trial;
who are demanding
when tribulation comes upon them,
and are blinded and conceited
when comfort gives them latitude;

whose self overcomes them with imaginations,
and who do not master the self by certainties;
who fear for others
on account of relatively insignificant misdeeds,
while expecting more for themselves
than what they have done;
who are seduced into wantonness
if they become rich,
and become despondent and lose heart
if they become poor;
who are inadequate when they work,
and overdo it when they ask;
who are first to be refractory
whenever a craving occurs to them,
and put off repentance and turning away from that;
who jump the track of religion
when tribulation strikes them;
who extol exemplars
but do not take a lesson from them,
and deliver sermons
without taking them to heart,
and thus are presumptuous in speech
but short on action;
who compete for what perishes
and give up what endures;
who see gain as loss and loss as gain;
who are afraid of death
yet do not hasten to escape;

who attach great importance
to insubordination from others
where they think little
of even more from themselves,
and make a big thing
of their own obedience
where they scorn the obedience of others,
so they discredit others
while flattering themselves;
who prefer diversion with the rich
to prayer with the poor;
who judge against others
in their own favor,
but never judge against themselves
in favor of others;
who give directions to others
while misguiding themselves,
so they command obedience
but are themselves astray,
and they demand in full
but do not give in full;
and who fear creation
for other than its Creator,
and do not fear the Creator
for the sake of the creation."

For every human being there is an end,
sweet or bitter.

Everyone who sets forth
eventually retreats.
And one retreats to where it is as if
one had never existed.

One who perseveres patiently
will not be without success,
even if it takes a long time.

Keep commitments
in all their integrity.

It is your responsibility to comply
with one whom you cannot excuse
on account of ignorance.

You have been shown,
if you see;
and you have been guided,
if you have found the way;
and you have been made to hear,
if you listen.

Reprove your brother
by being good to him,
and ward off his evil
by kindness to him.

Whoever puts himself
in places of passion
should not blame others
for having a bad opinion of him.

One who rules
claims a monopoly.

One who is headstrong and opinionated perishes,
while one who seeks the advice of others
becomes a partner in their understanding.

One who keeps his innermost thoughts secret
has the choice in his own hand.

Poverty is the greatest death.

One who acts fairly to someone
who does not do his own duty
is being servile to him.

There is no fault on a person
for postponement of his own right,
but there is blame on anyone
who takes what does not belong to him.

Complacency hinders growth.

The inevitable is near
and companionship little.

The dawn already gleams
for one with eyes.

It is easier to leave off wrongdoing
than to seek assistance.

Many a meal
prevents many meals.

People oppose
what they are ignorant about.

One who takes into consideration
all points of view
knows where the pitfalls are.

If you fear something
and it happens to you,
the intensity of the fear of it
is worse than what you feared.

The implement of leadership
is breadth of heart.

Repel what is offensive
by the garment of goodness.

Mow evil from the heart of another
by rooting it out of your own heart.

Obstinacy takes away judgment.

Greed is endless slavery.

The fruit of negligence
is remorse;
the fruit of judiciousness
is serenity.

There is no virtue
in not voicing good judgment,
just as there is no virtue
in speaking ignorantly.

When two biddings differ,
one of them is misleading.

I never doubted truth
after I was shown it.

I have not deceived
nor been deceived;

I have not gone astray
nor led anyone astray.

For one who initiates wrongdoing
there is remorse on the morrow.

The departure
is imminent.

Whoever turns away from truth perishes.

Man in this world
is nothing but a target
contested by every way of death,
and prey fallen upon
by every misfortune.
With every swallow of drink
there is gagging,
and with every bite of food
there is choking.
And no one gets anything
but at the cost of something else,
and no one greets a new day of life
without having lost another day of life.

So we are assistants of fate,
and our selves are a target of death.
So where can you expect permanence
when the night and the day
do not promote anything
without soon turning around
and attacking and destroying
what they have built,
scattering what they have brought together?

Son of Adam,
whatever you earn
beyond your upkeep
you are storing
for somebody else.

Hearts are in fact desirous,
preoccupied,
and flighty,
so approach them
by way of their desires
and their preoccupations,
for the heart goes blind
when it is coerced.

When will my wrath be soothed
if I am angered?
When I am incapable of vengeance
and told I should forbear,
or when I am capable of it
and told I should forgive?

Walking past filth on a dungheap,
Ḥaḍrat ʻAlī said,
"This is what misers scrimp for!"
It is also related that he said,
"This is what will remain on the morrow
of what you have been competing for!"

Nothing that teaches you a lesson
is lost from your wealth.

These hearts weary
as the bodies weary,
so seek for them
rarities of wisdom.

Once, on the edge of a crowd,
Ḥaḍrat ʻAlī said,

"They are those who prevail
when they join together
and are invisible when scattered."
It is also related, however,
that Ḥaḍrat 'Alī said,
"They are those who do ill
when they gather together
and do good when they separate."
It was said to him,
"We know the ill of their gathering,
but what is the good of their separation?"
Ḥaḍrat 'Alī replied,
"The workers return to their jobs,
and the people benefit from them,
like the return
of the builder to building,
of the weaver to weaving,
and of the baker to baking."

When a crook was brought to him
along with a noisy crowd,
Ḥaḍrat 'Alī said,
"There is no welcome for a face
seen only on bad occasions."

Do not under any circumstances
let the ungrateful cause you
to abstain from good work,
for sometimes one who enjoys nothing of it
thanks you for it;
and you may gain more
from the gratitude of the grateful
than from the neglect of the ungrateful.
And God loves the good.

All containers are reduced in capacity
by what is placed in them,
except a container of knowledge,
which expands.

The first compensation
of the insightful and patient one
for his understanding and tolerance
is that the people side with him
against the ignoramus.

If you are not patient,
then try to be like one who is patient,
for seldom does anyone imitate people
without verging on being one of them.

One who takes account of his self profits,
while one who neglects it loses.
And one who fears is safe,
and one who heeds a warning is discerning.
One who is discerning understands,
and one who understands knows.

Generosity is the protector
of good reputations,
while knowledge is the silencer
of fools.
Pardon is the tax on victory,
while consolation is your compensation
from betrayers.
Consultation is a source of guidance,
and one who thinks his own view enough
runs a risk.
Patience makes calamity fade,
while anxiety is one of the helpers of fate.
The most noble wealth
is to give up objects of desire,
and much intelligence is captive
to compulsive fancy.
One form of success
is remembering experience.

Friendship is a profitable relationship,
and do not trust the disaffected.

A man's vanity
is one of the things
that inhibits
his intelligence.

Disregard annoyance and pain,
and you will always be happy.

One who is mild
rather than forceful
has greater capacity
for outreach.

Contradiction ruins advice.

One who gains success
becomes presumptuous.

Through changes in circumstances
the essence of individuals is known.

Envy of the good
is an affliction in friendship.

Most things antagonistic to reason
are under the lightning flashes of ambition.

A judgment on a trust
made on the basis of supposition
is not just.

The worst of provisions for the Hereafter
is aggression toward people.

Among the noblest deeds
of the generous man
is his ignoring
of what he knows.

When someone is clothed
in the raiment of modesty,
the people do not see his faults.

By much silence,
there comes to be awe.
By justice,
communications increase.
By generosity,
worth grows.
By humility,
blessings come about.
By taking burdens upon oneself,
one attains leadership.
By just behavior,
enemies are overcome.
By forbearance in face of a fool,
helpers against him increase.

It is amazing how the envious
pay no attention to physical health.

The greedy one
is in the shackles
of abasement.

Contentment is kingdom enough;
goodness of character
is prosperity enough.

Form partnerships with those
who have abundant income,
for they are fitter for wealth
and better suited to its reduction.

One who gives a little
is given a lot.

Ḥaḍrat 'Alī said to his son Ḥasan,
"Do not call to combat
but respond if you are called to it,
for the provocateur is an oppressor,
and an oppressor is to be felled."

When answers compete,
correctness is concealed.

When capacity increases,
eagerness decreases.

Beware of the flight of blessings,
for nothing that runs away is returned.

Generosity awakens affection
more than kinship does.

If anyone thinks well of you,
then make his opinion true.

The most gracious deed
is the one
you have to force yourself to do.

Asked to characterize the intelligent,
Ḥaḍrat 'Alī said,
"That is the one
who puts things
in their proper places."
Asked to characterize the ignoramus,

Ḥaḍrat ʻAlī said,
"I have already done so."

One who follows the hesitant
loses rights,
and one who follows the slanderer
loses true friends.

A single stone in a house
that has been taken unjustly
is a guarantee of its ruin.

The day of the oppressed
against the oppressor
is more severe
than the day of the oppressor
against the oppressed.

O son of Adam!
Be your own administrator
in respect to your wealth,
and do with it what you wish
would be done with it
after your passing.

Rage is a kind of madness,
because the sufferer is regretful,
so if he is not regretful,
that means his madness
is ingrained.

Physical health comes
from having little envy.

One who has authority
is like someone riding on a lion;
he is envied for his position,
but he knows his situation better.

Treat the progeny of others well,
and you will be secure
in respect to your own progeny.

The speech of pundits is therapeutic
if what they say is correct,
but it is unhealthy
if what they say is mistaken.

O son of Adam!
Do not impose the concern
of the day that has not come
upon the day that has come,
for if it is part of your life,
God will bring you
your livelihood on that day.

Love your friend with some reserve,
for he might become inimical to you someday.
Despise your enemy with some reserve,
for he might become your friend someday.

Do not make your knowledge into ignorance
and your certainty into doubt.
When you know, act;
and when you are certain, proceed.

Greed motivates without producing
and guarantees without fulfilling.
Many a drinker of water chokes
before his thirst is quenched,
and the greater the importance

of that for which one vies,
the greater the calamity
of losing it.
Longing blinds the eye of insight,
and good luck comes to the one
who does not come after it.

A little bit at which you persevere
is better than a lot at which you are bored.

One who bears in mind
the distance of the journey
prospers.

Reflection is not like seeing with the eyes,
for the eyes may lie to their owner,
while the intellect does not deceive
one who asks for advice.

The ignorant among you are promoted,
while the knowledgeable are put off.

Knowledge cuts through
the excuse of malingerers.

Everyone who is being overtaken by death
asks for more time,
while everyone who still has time
makes excuses for procrastination.

For everything the people declare to be good,
fate conceals a day of evil.

Do not associate with a fool,
because he presents his behavior
in a favorable light
and wishes you would be like him.

You have three friends and three enemies.
Your friends are
your friend,
the friend of your friend,
and the enemy of your enemy.
Your enemies are
your enemy,
the enemy of your friend,
and the friend of your enemy.

When he saw a man striving against an enemy
by means harmful to himself,

Ḥaḍrat ‘Alī said,
“You are like one who pierces himself
in order to kill the one behind him.”

How many lessons there are,
and how little they are taken!

One who goes too far in argument errs,
while one who does not go far enough is oppressed,
and it is impossible for a quarreler
to be conscientious toward Truth.

People are children of the world,
and no one is blamed
for loving his mother.

An earnest man
never goes whoring.

The inevitability of death
is the best overseer.

People sleep in bereavement
but not in rage.

Friendship of fathers
means kinship among their sons,
and kinship is more in need of friendship
than is friendship in need of kinship.

Hearts do advance and retreat,
so when your heart advances,
give it more to do,
and when it retreats,
restrict it to obligatory duties.

Throw the stone back
from where it came,
for evil cannot be repelled
but by evil.

When asked how he overcame his opponents,
Ḥaḍrat ʻAlī explained,
"I never met any man
who did not help me against himself."

To someone who asked a puzzling question,
Ḥaḍrat 'Alī replied,
"Question in such a way
that a clear picture is obtained,
not in a nitpicking,
bothersome way.
For the ignorant one who seeks knowledge
is like the knower,
while the haphazard intellectual
is like the ignoramus
with his bothersome nitpicking."

Not to be in need of an excuse
is more powerful
than to be candid with an excuse.

One who is asked a request
is free until promising.

Knowledge is of two kinds,
that which is absorbed
and that which is heard.
And that which is heard

does not profit
if it is not absorbed.

Correctness of opinion goes along
with changes of the times;
it comes with them
and goes with them.

The day of justice
against the oppressor
is more severe
than the day of tyranny
against the oppressed.

The greatest wealth
is unconcern
with people's possessions.

Sayings are kept in memory,
inner thoughts are tried,
and every self is hostage
to what it has earned.
People are imperfect and weak,
except those whom God renders immune.

The questioner among them
is a troublemaker,
and the one of them who answers
is a sham.
The best of them in ideas
may even be turned back
from the best of his ideas
by pleasure or displeasure,
and the firmest of them in strength
may even be hurt by a look
or changed by a single statement.

One kind of protection
is unfeasibility of sin.

Your dignity is solid,
but making requests
evaporates it.
So be careful
about who it is
before whom you allow
your dignity to evaporate.

Praise that is more than deserved
is flattery,

while less than is deserved
indicates incapacity of expression
or else jealousy.

The most serious misdeed
is that which the perpetrator
thinks insignificant.

One who examines his own flaws
is distracted from the flaws of others,
and one who is satisfied
with the sustenance God grants him
does not grieve over what he has missed.
One who draws the sword of injustice
is killed by it.
One who merely suffers through things perishes,
but one who plunges into the depths of the sea
founders and drowns.
One who goes to places of ill repute
shows himself to be full of lust.
One who talks a lot increases in errors,
and one who increases in errors
becomes more shameless.
One who is shameless becomes imprudent,
and one who lacks prudence dies at heart;
one whose heart dies goes to hell.

And one who views people's flaws
and disapproves of them
but then accepts them in himself
is a real fool.
Contentment is wealth
that does not run out.
One who remembers death a lot
will be easily contented
with the simple things in life.
And one who knows
that his speech is part of his action
will speak little
except of that which concerns him.

There are three indications of an oppressor:
he oppresses those above him
by insubordination,
he oppresses those below him
by being domineering,
and he supports other oppressors.

The biggest fault
is to find fault with others
when you are like that too.

Captives of desire, desist,
for one who is attached to the world
is not scared by anything
but the screech of misfortune.
People, assume your own responsibility
for disciplining and refining your selves,
deflecting them from their habits.

Do not think of anyone's statement as evil
if you can find it capable of bearing good.

Anyone who wishes to keep his dignity
should give up disputation.

Stupidity includes hurrying
before the right time
and waiting until
the opportunity has passed.

Do not ask about
what does not exist,
for there is work for you
in what does exist.

Contemplation is a clear mirror,
consideration is a sincere cautioner,
and adequate culture for your self
is for it to keep you away
from what you detest in others.

Knowledge is linked to action,
so one who knows acts,
as knowledge calls for action
and will depart
if it is not answered.

Truth is weighty but wholesome;
falsehood is light but poisonous.

Stinginess combines similar defects,
for it is a bridle that leads to all evils.

Words are under your control
until you have spoken them,
but you come under their control
once you have spoken them.

So guard your tongue
as you guard your gold,
for many a word
snatches away blessings
and brings adversity.

Do not say
what you do not know,
but neither say all
of what you do know.

To lean upon the world
and what you see of it
is ignorance,
to abridge good work
when you are confident of reward for it
is cheating,
and to repose trust in everyone
before examination or testing
is weakness.

Whoever seeks something gets it,
or part of it.

Poverty is indeed a trial,
but sickness is worse than poverty.
And worse than sickness of the body
is sickness of the heart.
Wealth is indeed a blessing,
but physical health is better than wealth.
And even better than physical health
is soundness of heart.

Speak, and be known,
for a man is hidden
under his tongue.

Take of the world
what comes to you,
and turn away from
what turns away from you.
If you cannot do this,
at least be decent in seeking.

Many a spoken word
is more piercing than an attack.

Everything with which one is content
is sufficient.

Prefer death to disgrace.
Be content with little
rather than curry favor.
One who would not
receive something anyway
would not get it
by contrivance.
Destiny is two days,
one for you
and one against you,
so when it is for you,
do not be proud or reckless,
and when it is against you,
then be patient.

Put aside your pride,
set down your arrogance,
and remember your grave.

Truth will throw down
anyone who fights with it.

The heart is the book
of perception.

Conscience is the head of character.

Endure with the patience
of the free,
or else forget with the forgetfulness
of the ingenuous.

Understanding is what makes relationships.

You are getting enough
from your intelligence
if it makes plain to you
the ways that lead you astray
from your integrity.

Do good without looking down
on anything involved in it.
For the small is great,
and little is much.
And let no one say
that someone else is fitter to act
than oneself,

for by God it will then be so.
For both good and evil
have their partisans,
so whichever of the two you abandon,
there will be plenty of its partisans
to make up for you.

Mildness is a protective covering,
and intelligence is a cutting sword.
So cover the flaws in your character
with mildness,
and battle your whims
with intelligence.

It is not appropriate for a mortal
to be confident of two qualities:
health and wealth.
One whom you saw healthy one moment
is suddenly taken ill,
and one whom you saw rich one moment
is suddenly bankrupt.

The man who gets the worst bargain
and is the most unsuccessful in his endeavors
is the one who wears out his body

in seeking his wealth
but is not assisted by destiny
toward his aim,
who leaves the world
with his sorrow and pain
and arrives at the Hereafter
bearing his responsibility.

Remember that enjoyments pass
while consequences remain.

The foremost of people is the one
by whom the high-minded are recognized.

Asked which is better, justice or generosity,
Ḥaḍrat ‘Alī said,
“Justice puts things in their places,
while generosity takes them out of their domains.
And justice is a common public guide,
while generosity is a special boon.
So justice is the more noble
and the better of the two.”

How sleep demolishes
the resolutions of the day!

When someone has a clear characteristic,
look closely for others like it.

One who regards the self as precious
attaches little importance to cravings.

Your turning away
from one who seeks of you
is reduction of fortune,
and your seeking of someone
who turns away from you
is self-degradation.

Rulerships are the racetracks of men.

Two avid devotees are never surfeited:
a seeker of knowledge,
and a seeker of the world.

Forbearance and patience
are consonant one with the other;

loftiness of aspiration
produces them both.

Faith rests on four pillars:
patience, certitude, justice, and struggle.
Patience, furthermore, is based on four disciplines:
yearning, apprehension, abstinence, and expectation.
So one who yearns for Paradise forgets desires,
and one who is on guard against Hellfire
turns aside from forbidden things.
One who is abstinent in this world
thinks lightly of misfortunes,
and one who expects death
hastens to good deeds.
Certitude is also based on four disciplines:
enlightenment of intelligence,
elucidation of wisdom,
spiritual counsel on what is important,
and following original norms.
Wisdom becomes clear
to whoever reflects on intelligence,
and whoever has wisdom become clear
knows what is important.
And whoever knows what is important
is in accord with original norms.
Justice is also based on four disciplines:
immersion in understanding,

penetration of knowledge,
brightness in judgment,
and firm establishment of thoughtfulness.
For one who understands
knows with penetrating knowledge,
and one who knows with penetrating knowledge
proceeds judiciously from the start.
And one who is thoughtful
has not been negligent of his trust
and lives a benign life among the people.
Struggle is also based on four disciplines:
the imperative to do what is right,
prohibition of wrong,
speaking truth at the appropriate times and places,
and attacking the vicious and iniquitous.
For one who commands what is right
strengthens the back of the faithful,
and one who forbids what is wrong
defies scoffers and oppressors.
And one who speaks the truth
at the appropriate times and places
has carried out his obligation,
and one who attacks the vicious and iniquitous
in defense of God
will be defended by God
and fulfilled by God
on the day of resurrection.

Disbelief rests on four pillars:
preoccupation, contention, perversion, and obstinacy.
For whoever is preoccupied
does not turn to truth,
and whoever contends ignorantly
persists in his blindness to truth.
And whoever is perverse
finds good vexatious
and thinks what is foul is fair,
becoming drunk with the intoxication of error.
And whoever is obstinate
finds his path become harder,
his business get more difficult,
and his way out become cramped.
Doubt, furthermore, is based on four things:
contentiousness, fear, irresoluteness, and capitulation.
For whoever habitually engages in disputation
will not see the dawn of his night,
and whoever fears what faces him
shrinks back and gives up his intention.
Whoever is irresolute in uncertainty
is trampled by the hooves of devils,
and whoever capitulates
to the perishing of this world and the next
perishes in them.

Do not approach extra observances
when they interfere with obligatory observances.

Ḥaḍrat 'Alī said to an ailing friend,
"May God make what you have suffered
a means of diminishing your sins.
For there is no reward in sickness,
but it diminishes sins and removes them
as it were like falling leaves.
There is only reward
in the speech of the tongue
and the work of the hands and feet.
And yet God the Glorified
admits to Paradise anyone, at will,
for truthfulness of intention
and goodness of innermost thoughts."

Blessed are they
who have remembered their ultimate destination,
who have acted with due consideration,
who have been content with sufficiency,
and who have been pleased with God.

Even if I struck the nose of a believer
with my sword to make him hate me,
he would not hate me;
and even if I showered a hypocrite

with all that is in the world to make him love me,
he would not love me.
And that is because it is decreed,
as definitively stated
by the Unlettered Prophet himself,
may God bless him and his family
and give them peace,
when he said,
" 'Alī, no believer will hate you,
and no hypocrite will love you."

An evil that repels you
is fairer in the sight of God
than a good deed that charms you.

Do not hope for anything but God,
and do not fear anything but your sin.
When asked about what you do not know,
do not be ashamed to say you do not know;
and when you do not know something,
do not be embarrassed to learn it.
And may you have patience,
for patience is to faith
as the head is to the body;
there is no good in a body without its head,
and none in faith without patience.

For those who put in order
what is between them and God,
God will put in order
what is between them and other people.
And for those who put in order
their task for the Hereafter,
God puts in order
their business in this world.
And those who have caution from themselves
have protection from God.

An expert jurisprudent is one
who does not cause people to despair of God's mercy,
does not cause them to lose hope of refreshment from
God,
and does not cause them to feel exempt from the design
of God.

Let none of you say,
"O God, I seek refuge with You from trouble,"
because the fact is that there is no one
who is not involved in trouble.
But whoever would seek protection
should seek protection

from troubles that lead astray.
For God the Glorified says,
"Realize that your wealth and your children are a trial."
And the meaning of this
is that God tests them by their wealth
and their children
to make it clear
who is discontent with his sustenance
and who is content with his lot,
even though God knows them better
than they do themselves;
it is to allow the manifestation of the deeds
by which reward and punishment are earned,
for some of them like to have male offspring
and dislike to have females,
and some of them love material gain
and hate discredit to their status.

Ḥaḍrat 'Alī was asked what good is. He said,
"Good is not that your possessions and children increase,
but good is that your knowledge increases
and your insight grows more powerful,
and that the people are proud to serve your God.
For when you do good, you praise God,
and when you make peace,
you seek the forgiveness of God.
And there are none who are good in this world but two:

one who commits sins but makes amends for
them by repentance,
and one who is quick to do good deeds."

Among ways of atonement for major sins
are helping the troubled
and comforting the distressed.

O son of Adam!
When you see God
following you with blessings
even though you are disobedient,
watch out!

Beware, beware!
For God has been so protective
that it almost seems like divine forgiveness.

A conscientious act is not insignificant,
for how can what has been accepted be insignificant?

The closest people to the prophets
are those most knowledgeable about what they brought.

The Qur'ān says, "The closest people to Abraham
are those who follow him and this Prophet,
and those who believe."
Indeed, the friend of Muḥammad
is whoever obeys God,
even if the relationship is remote,
and the enemy of Muḥammad
is whoever defies God,
even if the relationship is close.

Sleep in a state of certainty
is better than prayer in a state of doubt.

Hearing someone recite from the Qur'ān,
"We belong to God, and to God we will return,"
Ḥaḍrat 'Alī remarked,
"When we say, 'We belong to God,'
we admit our subordination,
and when we say, 'We return to God,'
we admit our mortality."

When people praised him to his face, Ḥaḍrat 'Alī said,
"O God, You know me better than I do myself,
and I know myself better than they do.
O God, make us better

than they think we are,
and forgive us what they do not know."

Ḥaḍrat 'Alī was seen in a patched garment
and remark was made to him about it.
Ḥaḍrat 'Alī said,
"The heart becomes docile on its account,
the self becomes humble thereby,
and the believers take to it.
For this world and the next
are irreconcilable enemies, different paths.
So whoever loves this world and befriends it
hates the Hereafter and regards it an enemy.
They are as east and west,
with someone walking in between:
every step closer to one
is a step further away from the other."

Late one night, gazing at the stars, Ḥaḍrat 'Alī said,
"Blessed are those
who are abstemious in this world
out of desire for the Hereafter.
They are a people
who take the earth for a carpet,
its dust for a bed,
and its water for perfume;

they take the Qur'ān for a watchword
and prayer for a covering.
And they impose a blockade on the world
in the manner of the Messiah.
Indeed, David, peace be upon him,
rose by night and said,
'This is an hour at which
anyone who calls on God is answered,
except for a tax collector,
an intelligence agent,
a police officer,
or a tambourinist or a drummer.' "

God has prescribed precepts for you
that you should not thwart,
and has delineated boundaries for you
that you should not cross,
and has forbidden things to you
that you should not violate,
and has been silent to you,
though not out of forgetfulness,
about things that you should not take up.

Whenever people omit any of their religious obligations
to cultivate their worldly affairs,
God inflicts something worse on them.

No one establishes the order
of God the Glorified
except one who does not flatter,
is not a conformist,
and is not subordinate to objects of desire.

How many are lured to destruction
by being treated well,
are beguiled by being shielded,
and are seduced by being well spoken of!
None of God's trials are as trying as fulfillment.

I relate the lineage of Islam
as no one has related it before me.
Islam is surrender,
and surrender is certitude;
certitude is authentication,
and authentication is assurance;
assurance is realization,
and realization is work.

I wonder at the miser
who hastens to poverty,

leaving behind the very wealth he seeks,
for he lives in this world like a pauper
but will have to settle his account in the Hereafter like
the rich.
And I wonder at the proud one,
who was a drop of sperm yesterday
and will be a rotting corpse tomorrow.
And I wonder at the one who doubts God
even though he sees God's creation.
And I wonder at the one who forgets death
even though he sees the dead.
And I wonder at the one who disavows the final genesis
even though he sees the original genesis.
And I wonder at one who takes up residence
in the abode of annihilation,
abandoning the abode of permanence.

The majesty of the Creator in your eyes
diminishes created things in your eyes.

There is an angel of God
who calls out every night,
"Reproduce for death,
accumulate for destruction,
and build for demolition."

Whoever is granted four things
is not denied four things.
Whoever is granted prayer
is not denied response.
Whoever is granted repentance
is not denied acceptance.
Whoever is allowed to seek forgiveness
is not denied forgiveness.
Whoever is granted gratitude
is not denied increase.

Prayer is the offering of the conscientious.
Pilgrimage is the struggle of the weak.
There is a tax on everything,
and the tax on the body is sleep.
The struggle of a woman
is to treat her husband well.

Help descends according to necessity.

How many of those who fast
have nothing to their fast
but hunger and thirst!
And how many of those who pray
have nothing to their prayer

but sleeplessness and toil!
How nice in comparison
are the sleep and the breakfast of the sagacious!

Govern your faith by charity,
make your wealth inviolable by paying the poor tax,
and repulse the waves of tribulation by prayer.

Once Ḥaḍrat 'Alī took Kumail ibn Ziyād to a graveyard;
when it was deserted, he heaved a deep sigh and said,
"Kumail, these hearts are containers,
and the best of them are the most heedful of them.
So remember what I am going to tell you.
There are three kinds of people.
One is the learned one who is godly,
another is the learner who is on the road to deliverance.
And then there are the uncultivated riffraff
who follow every cawing,
bending with every wind;
they do not seek enlightenment
by the light of knowledge,
and do not resort
to a reliable support.
Kumail, knowledge is better than wealth.
Knowledge protects you,

while you protect wealth.
Wealth is diminished by spending,
while knowledge grows by use.
Kumail, knowledge is a religion
to which one is indebted;
by it humanity acquires strength in life
and beauty in speech
when it has been fulfilled.
Knowledge is the ruler,
while wealth is the ruled.
Kumail, those who accumulate wealth
have perished even though they are alive,
while those with knowledge
last as long as time;
their individualities may be gone,
but their example exists in hearts.
Here (and he pointed to his heart)
I have abundant knowledge,
if only I could find people to bear it.
Unfortunately,
I have found learners who are not faithful to it,
applying it to the devices of belief in the world,
gaining the upper hand over God's servants
by means of the bounty of God,
domineering God's friends by its authority;
or those who find fault with bearers of truth
without having any insight of their own.
Doubt sparks in their hearts

at the first sign of uncertainty.
Indeed, there is neither this nor that!
Either they are greedy for enjoyment,
submitting to the fetters of craving,
or they are infatuated with collecting a hoard;
neither type cares at all for religion,
resembling freely grazing cattle in their ways.
Thus does knowledge die out
with the passing of its bearers.
O God! Certainly the earth is not devoid
of those who rise in honor of God for good reason,
either openly and notably
or in fear and obscurity,
so that the proof and clarifications of God
may not be in vain.
But how many are they,
and where are they?
They are, by God, fewest in number
but greatest in rank with God.
By them God preserves
the divine proofs and clarifications
until they entrust them
to others like them
and plant them in the hearts
of others like them.
By them knowledge enters into real insight,
and they are imbued with the spirit of certainty.
They consider easy what seems hard

to those who lead a life of comfort,
and they take to
what the ignorant are averse to.
They are physically in the world,
yet their spirits are suspended
in the highest liberation.
They are the deputies of God on earth,
and are those who invite people
to the religion of God.
Oh, how I long to see them!"

Do not obey creatures
in defiance of the Creator.

One who sharpens
the spearhead of anger
in defense of God
grows strong in the killing
of militant falsehood.

When he heard the saying of the Seceders,
"Decision is God's alone,"
Ḥaḍrat 'Alī said,
"The statement is true,
but falsehood is conceived of it."

With every human being
there are two guarding angels,
and when fate comes,
they open a way
between it and the individual.
Indeed, destiny
is an invulnerable shelter.

People, fear God,
who hears when you speak
and knows when you keep a secret.
And be mindful of death,
which overtakes you
even if you flee it,
seizes you if you stay put,
and remembers you
even if you forget it.

Be wary of God
in the manner of one
who prepares without distraction
and makes every effort at preparation,
who concentrates while there is time
and hastens out of dread,

who considers the recurrence of troubles,
the outcome of the beginning,
and the ultimate end.

Asked about faith,
Ḥaḍrat ʻAlī said,
"Faith is experience
by the heart,
avowal by the tongue,
and action by the limbs."

One who is aggrieved at the world
is discontent with the judgment of God,
and one who complains
about misfortunes that befall him
is complaining about his Lord.
One who approaches a rich man
and abases himself to him
because of his riches
loses a third of his religion.
One who reads the Qurʻān
yet falls into Hellfire when he dies
was one of those
who took the signs of God as a joke.
One whose heart is stuck
to love of the world

finds three things from it
stuck to his heart:
uneasiness that is never absent from him,
desire that never leaves him,
and expectations that are never completely fulfilled.

Asked about
the statement of God,
"We will make them live
a good life,"
Ḥaḍrat 'Alī said,
"That refers to contentment."

The Exalted has said,
"God commands justice and goodness."
Justice is fairness,
and goodness is kindness.

By God,
this world of yours
is more worthless in my eyes
than pig entrails
in the hand of a leper.

If people worship God out of desire,
that is the worship of merchants.
If people worship God out of fear,
that is the worship of slaves.
If people worship God out of gratitude,
that is the worship of the free.

Fear God with some awe,
even if it be a little,
and place a protective screen
between you and God,
even if it be thin.

God has a right in every blessing,
and whoever discharges that
is given more from it,
and whoever shorts that right
is in danger of losing the blessing.

I know God the Glorified
by the nullification of resolutions,
the unraveling of arrangements,
and the invalidation of intentions.

The bitterness of this world
is the sweetness of the Hereafter,
and the sweetness of this world
is the bitterness of the Hereafter.

God prescribes
faith unadulterated by idolatry,
prayer unblemished by pride,
poor tax produced to provide livelihood,
fasting as a test of sincerity of character,
pilgrimage to facilitate the understanding of religion,
struggle for the honor of surrender to God,
enjoining good for the improvement of the people,
forbidding evil to deter the foolish,
keeping relations with kinfolk to increase number,
retaliatory punishment to spare bloodshed,
establishment of ordinances
to underline the importance of prohibitions,
avoiding alcoholic drinks
for the improvement of intelligence,
avoidance of stealing
to fulfill the requirements of integrity and decency,
avoiding adultery to safeguard descent,
avoiding sodomy to increase progeny,
testifying as a witness to help out in disputes,
avoidance of lying to honor truthfulness,
peacefulness as security from fear,

reliability for the integrity of the social fabric,
and obedience out of respect for leadership.

Ḥaḍrat 'Alī said to Kumail,
"Tell your people to set out
to acquire noble traits
and to effect the needs
of those who sleep.
For by God,
whose hearing extends
to all voices,
whenever anyone
gladdens a heart,
God creates for him
a grace from his gladness
that runs to him
when misfortune befalls
like water running down a slope,
so that it drives misfortune away
as wild animals are driven away."

When you are reduced to poverty,
use charity to trade with God.

Fidelity to the treacherous
is treachery to God,

and treachery to the treacherous
is fidelity to God.

How many
have been lured into destruction
by being well treated,
have been misled
by being protected,
have been seduced
by being well spoken of!
God the Glorified tries no one
with a trial like fulfillment.

Someone asked Ḥaḍrat ‘Alī
to define faith for him.
‘Alī said,
“Come to me tomorrow
so that I may tell you
in the hearing of the people;
thus if you forget what I say,
another may remember it for you.
For a saying is like a fugitive,
which one person may track down,
while another may allow it to escape.”

People work in the world in two ways.
There is the worker of work
in the world for the world,
whose work preoccupies him
and distracts him from his ultimate destiny;
he fears poverty for his posterity
but feels safe for himself.
So he consumes his life
to the profit of others.
Then there is the worker of work
in the world for what is after it,
to whom things of the world come
without working for them,
so one achieves twofold fortune at once
and possesses both the two houses.
One becomes eminent
in the sight of God,
and God does not deny
any need one requests.

Know with certain knowledge
that God does not grant any mortal
—no matter how great his strategy,
no matter how intense his seeking,
and no matter how powerful his machinations—
more than what is determined
in the Recollection of Wisdom.

And God does not withhold from any mortal,
on account of weakness or lack of wiles,
what it is determined shall come to him
according to the Recollection of Wisdom.
And the one who knows this
and acts on it
is the most comfortable of people
with the yield of what is useful,
while the one who rejects and doubts it
is the most troubled of people
with the detriment of what is harmful.
And many of the advantaged
are being lured into destruction
by advantages,
while many of the afflicted
are being affected constructively
by affliction.
So increase your gratefulness,
O hearer,
and reduce your haste,
and stay within the limitations
of your income.

O God!
I take refuge with You
from appearing to the public
to be better than I am

while my inner mind
is repulsive to You
for what it conceals,
preventing the people
from lamenting over me
for all that You know of me,
for I would be showing the people
a fine exterior
while informing You
of the evil of my actions,
drawing near to mortals
while distancing myself
from Your favor.

Between you and spiritual counsel
is a veil of heedlessness.

Asked about Destiny,
Ḥaḍrat 'Alī said,
"It is a dark path;
do not enter upon it.
It is a deep sea;
do not plunge into it.
It is a secret of God;
do not burden yourself with it."

When disowning a servant,
God denies him knowledge.

In the past I had a brother in God:
the insignificance of the world in his eyes
made him great in my eyes.
He was not ruled by his stomach,
he did not wish for what he did not have,
and he did not seek more of what he did have.
He used to keep silent much of the time,
and when he spoke he silenced all speakers
and quenched the thirst of all questioners.
He was delicate and considered weak,
but when an emergency arose
he was a veritable lion of the forest,
a viper of the valley.
He would not advance an argument
unless it was decisive,
and he would not censure anyone
for what could be excused
until he had heard the excuse.
He did not complain of a pain
until he recovered.
He used to say what he would do
and not say what he would not do.
If he was ever defeated in speech,
yet he was never defeated in silence.

He was more eager to listen than to speak.
When two things came to him,
he would see which was more emotionally desirable
and then do the contrary.
These qualities of character
are incumbent upon you,
so adhere to them
and try to excel one another in them.
For even if you are not capable of them,
know that to take a little is better
than to leave the lot.

Even if God did not threaten the disobedient,
one would be obliged not to disobey God
out of gratitude for the blessings of God.

Ḥaḍrat 'Alī was asked,
"How can God call all creatures to account,
many as they are?"
'Alī replied,
"Just as God sustains them,
many as they are."
He was then asked,
"How can God call all creatures to account
without being seen by them?"
'Alī replied,

"Just as God sustains them
without being seen by them."

The afflicted one whose trial is severe
is not more in need of prayer
than the one who is spared
but not immune to affliction.

The indigent one is actually
a messenger of God,
so whoever denies the poor
denies God,
and whoever gives to the poor
gives to God.

Beware the opinions of the faithful,
for God has put truth on their tongues.

The faith of a mortal does not hold true
until one is more sure
of what is in the hand of God
than one is
of what is in one's own hand.

In the Qur'ān
is report of the past,
information on the future,
and wisdom for the meanwhile.

I am the leader of the faithful,
while money is the leader of profligates.

When he passed by those of the Seceders
who had been killed in the battle of Nahrawān,*
Ḥaḍrat 'Alī said,
"Woe to you!
The one who harmed you
was the one who deceived you."
He was asked,
"Who deceived them,
O Commander of the Faithful?"
Ḥaḍrat 'Alī replied,
"Satan the deluder,
and their own selves,

*The battle of Nahrawān was fought against the Seceders, who opposed 'Alī. Although they were defeated, one of the surviving Seceders ultimately assassinated 'Alī.

with compulsive tendencies to evil;
they deceived them with longings
and disjointed them with sins,
promised them victories,
then hurled them into Hell."

Beware of disobeying God when alone,
for the witness is the Judge.

The age up to which
God allows mortals
to have an excuse
is sixty years.

One whom sin overcomes
does not succeed,
and one who prevails by evil
is defeated.

God the Glorified has ordained
the support of the poor
in the wealth of the rich,
so no indigent goes hungry
but for what a rich man enjoys.

And God Most High
will question them about that.

The least of your duties to God
is that you do not use God's blessings
to help you do wrong.

God the Glorified has made obedience
a prize for the more able
where the incapable are negligent.

Ḥaḍrat 'Alī described a believer thus:
"A believer has his joy on his face
and his sorrow in his heart.
He is most magnanimous
and yet most humble;
he dislikes high rank
and hates renown.
His sorrow is long,
his concern far-reaching.
He is often silent,
and his time is occupied.
He is grateful, patient,
immersed in thought,
sparing in making requests,

even-tempered and mild,
firmer than rock
yet humbler than a slave."

If a mortal saw
the end of his life
and his final destination,
he would loathe
desire and its deceptions.

One who prays
but does no work
is as one who shoots
without a bowstring.

O societies of people!
Be aware of God!
So many entertain hopes
of what they do not attain,
build houses they do not live in,
and amass that which
they are going to leave behind them.
One may have gotten something wrongly,
or by denying a right;
having come upon it

in an unlawful manner,
one bears the weight
of sins on its account.
So one returns with this heavy load
and arrives before God
regretful and sorrowful.
One loses this world
and the Hereafter;
that is clearly a loss!

One kind of protection
is unfeasibility of sin.

O people!
Let God see you
as fearful in good times
as God sees you
frightened in calamity.
For whoever is enriched
but does not see this as gradual seduction
feels safe from what is to be feared,
and whoever is impoverished
but does not see it as a trial
loses hope.

God has ordained parameters
for all of your limbs,
in reference to which
they will testify about you
on the day of resurrection.

Beware lest God see you
being rebellious toward God
or missing an opportunity to obey God,
for you will be the loser.
So when you are strong,
be strong in obedience to God,
and when you are weak,
be weak in rebelling against God.

One of the things
that make the world contemptible
is that God is defied only therein,
and what is with God is granted
only on the condition of renouncing it.

There is no good
in good followed by Hellfire,
and there is no calamity
in calamity followed by Paradise.

Every felicity other than Paradise is lowly,
and every trial outside of Hell is well-being.

Be abstemious in the world,
and God will show you its defects.
And do not be negligent,
for you will not be neglected.

How good it is for the rich
to be humble to the poor,
seeking reward from God;
but even better than that
is the haughtiness of the poor
toward the rich,
trusting in God.

God does not entrust
anyone with intelligence
without saving him thereby someday.

Do not use the sharpness of your tongue
against the One who gave you the power of speech,
or the eloquence of your speech
against the One who guided you.

The world deceives,
causes harm,
and passes away;
God has not approved it
either as a reward for saints
or as an obstacle for sinners.
Indeed, partisans of the world
are like a caravan all decked out;
when their driver calls,
off they go!

Wretched is the son of Adam:
fate is sealed,
causes are hidden,
works are preserved;
insects are after him,
choking kills him,
sweat makes him stink!

For those who make
their inner thoughts wholesome,
God will make
their outward manifestations wholesome.
For those who work

on God's religion,
God will assure them
of sufficiency in their worldly affairs.
And for those who do right
in their relationship with God,
God will improve their relationships
with other people.

There are servants of God
whom God favors with blessings
for the service of others
and whom God keeps supplied
as long as they are generous
with what they have.
For if they refuse or withhold,
God takes those favors away from them
and transfers them to others.

Whoever complains of a need
to a believer
is as if complaining to God,
and whoever complains of it
to a disbeliever
is as if complaining *about* God.

A holiday is only a holiday
for one whose fast God accepts
and whose prayer God thanks.
And every day
on which God is not disobeyed
is itself a holiday.

Abstinence is all in two sayings
from the Qur'ān:
"May you not be grieved
over what is lost to you,
and do not exult
at what has been given you."
For whoever does not grieve
over what is gone
and does not exult
at what comes
has grasped abstinence
from both ends.

Anyone who makes much
of small misfortunes
God will try
with greater ones.

Is there no free individual
who will leave this unswallowed morsel
to those who are attached to it?
There is no price for your selves but Paradise,
so do not sell them for anything else.

Faith means that you prefer
truth when it hurts you
to falsehood when it profits you,
and that there is nothing in your speech
that is beyond your action,
and that you be wary of God
when you talk about others.

The world was created
for other than it;
it was not created for itself.

Asked about Unification and Justice,
Ḥaḍrat 'Alī said,
"Unification means you do not
entertain any imagination about God,
and Justice means that you do not
entertain any suspicions about God."

A martyr in the cause of God
does not have a greater reward
than one who has means
but abstains from indulgence.
Indeed, one who is pure
is virtually one of the angels.

God does not oblige the ignorant to learn
until having obliged the learned to teach.